A BOOK OF COMFORT

A BOOK OF COMFORT
For Those in Sickness

P. B. POWER, M.A.

THE BANNER OF TRUTH TRUST

THE BANNER OF TRUTH TRUST
3 Murrayfield Road, Edinburgh EH12 6EL
PO Box 652, Carlisle, Pennsylvania 17013, USA

*

First Banner of Truth
Trust reprint 1974

ISBN 0 85151 203 8

*

Printed and bound in Great Britain
by Hazell Watson & Viney Ltd,
Aylesbury, Bucks

Contents

INTRODUCTION

Amongst the many wonderful truths which are spoken of God in the Bible, one of the most wonderful and beautiful is that He is a 'God of comfort.'

'Comfort' is such a soothing word in itself that, the moment we hear of it in connection with God, we are led to expect great things; some cheering, some lifting up, some refreshment, some ease, some lightening of our trouble, something very good.

There are sick-beds without God, and then of course there can be little comfort. No wonder that the days are long and dreary, and the nights full of blackness, when a man has to bear his trouble alone – when he has no God to talk to, no God to talk to him – when, if he does think of God at all, it is only with fear, lest this illness may bring him into His presence; or else with discontent, thinking that it is He who has laid this upon him.

These pages are not written for such as want to have a sick-bed without God, except indeed to show them a more excellent way.

Should this little book fall into the hands of such an one; then it says – 'Dear friend, you cannot help being ill, being in bed, or on the sofa, or even in an arm-chair (for many people on sofas, and in arm-chairs, are quite as ill, and quite as much to be pitied, and quite as much in need of comfort as those who cannot stir from their beds) but you can help being as unhappy as you are. All these circumstances *need* not be comfortless. They are so, only because you shut God out from them.'

But what about God being a God of comfort? Everything depends upon that. You, who do not look to Him, and you who do, are the one as badly off as the other, unless God be a God of comfort.

Now, for all our sakes, the first and best thing to do will be to see what His Word says about Him; because there first, and in the experiences of His people next, we are to find Him.

And if we find Him to be this God of comfort, then you have misjudged Him hitherto, when you thought Him an enemy, and unkind, and a judge, and an avenger, and nothing else; now, and henceforth, be encouraged to think of Him in a new light.

'Speak good of His name,' says the Psalmist. That is what I want to do in the forefront of this little book, because if you can be persuaded to think good of Him, you shall have all the benefits spoken of here; and I should like *every* sick one who reads these pages to get all the blessing, to be richly comforted.

Blessed Lord, this is *A Book of Comfort*; and that it may be so indeed, first we must be sure of what Thou art. O Thou most worthy Judge eternal, we have no comfort in ourselves, and unless Thou hadst revealed Thyself as a comforting God we could have had none in Thee. Thy justice, and power, and majesty are no comfort to us if they are alone, for we are only vile earth, and miserable sinners; it is what Thou tellest us of Thyself that gives us any joy. We would not presume to look for comfort in the direction of Thyself, if Thou hadst not pointed out to us the way; but now that Thou hast done this, from Thee, and the things concerning Thee alone, shall come our comfort and our peace.

Yes, from Thee, O Holy Ghost *the* Comforter, by whom the Father's peace pervades the soul. Show Thyself to us, as Thou art in Thy Word. Comfort us with the kindness that there is in Thyself; and speak peace to all the readers of this book, for the sake of the great Peacemaker, – the Prince of peace, Jesus Christ Himself – Amen.

1: IS GOD A GOD OF COMFORT AT ALL?

The question at the head of this chapter must be settled before this little book can be to its readers, what I earnestly desire it should be, that is, *A Book of Comfort*.

For many a sick man will say, 'The last place where I can seek for comfort is with God. Is not this the great God who is full of power and majesty? Is not this the One who made heaven and earth; why should I think that He will concern Himself about such small affairs as mine?' And even if we think that He will, we are inclined to say, 'Is not this the One I have offended, whose laws I have broken, whose calls I have rejected, who is of purer eyes than to behold iniquity? And when I call to mind what I have been, and what I am, surely He is the last one I ought to go to for comfort.'

All this is quite reasonable. I should not have a word to say against it. And I myself, instead of trying to write a 'comfort book,' should have to give myself up to entire despair, if it were not that God had told me certain things in His Word about Himself, which warrant me in making my 'comfort book;' and in saying to *every* one who reads it – 'It is all for you – all, my dear friend, without any abatement or reservation, all for you. God wills you to be comforted, and that comfort He wills you to have, by having Himself.'

So far from God's not willing you to come to Himself for comfort, what He speaks most plainly about, is against your going anywhere else. He knows you are in need of comfort, one from one cause, and another from another (every man's trouble is not the same, and even if it were the same, it does not touch on the same point precisely, or in the same way); but whatever it is, and however it works, the cry is that we should not forsake Him the fountain of living waters, and hew out for ourselves broken cisterns which can hold no water.

Scripture tells us that God is a jealous God; and He is not only jealous of a man's worshipping any other God, but of His being put second in anything; and, amongst other things, in comforting.

No doubt there is comfort to be had from friends, and from books, and from visits of ministers, and from many other sources, but they must all be put under God; otherwise they will be like Job's comforters – 'miserable comforters are ye all.' They will give way in some unexpected time and manner, and leave us with nothing, because we had not God.

But let us see from Holy Scripture how God Himself appears in this matter of comfort. Do we find Him very plainly here?

St. Paul tells us very plainly what God Himself is in this way.

He had just been wishing grace and peace,

two very comfortable things, to the Corinthian church; and where were these to come from? From God our Father, and from the Lord Jesus Christ. Then the apostle, as though he could not restrain himself when he came to speak of these good things as coming from the Father, breaks out into this grand ascription of praise to Him — 'Blessed be God, even the Father of our Lord Jesus Christ, the Father of mercies, and the God of all comfort; who comforteth us in all our tribulation.' [2 Cor. 1:2–4].

Then, farther on in chapter 12, verses 5 and 6, he gives us an example of how God comforted. The comfort came by a human hand; it came at a most seasonable time, for trials just then were very heavy, but it came from God; and Paul distinctly traced God in the way in which his comfort came. 'I am filled,' he says, 'with comfort; I am exceedingly joyful in all our tribulation. For when we were come into Macedonia, our flesh had no rest, but we were troubled on every side; without were fightings, within were fears. Nevertheless, God that comforteth those that are cast down, (note that phrase, it just suits you,) comforted us by the coming of Titus.'

God has His own times and ways of comforting. I would now only just draw your attention to the fact that the apostle speaks of Him as One who is in the habit of comforting those who are cast down. It comes in quite naturally, and not as something strange, and wonderful, and out of the way, which had happened here, but may never happen again.

Some people speak of God as though there is no comfort in Him at all; and that Jesus is to comfort us by enabling us to escape from God. But the apostle Paul saw the Father and the Son both one in this blessed work of comfort; and if there is no other verse in the Bible to comfort a poor soul, then the 16th and 17th verses of the 2nd chapter of 2 Thessalonians ought to do so; they ought to bring a man to God Himself for comfort. 'Now our Lord Jesus Christ Himself, and God, even our Father which hath loved us, and hath given us everlasting consolation and good hope through grace, comfort your hearts, and stablish you in every good word and work.'

The Psalmist, a man, as you know, of many troubles, found his comfort in God Himself; not in running away from Him, but in coming to Him. It was upon what God said that David relied; and if that had not been something comfortable, it would have been of no use to him. 'Remember the word unto Thy servant, upon which Thou hast caused me to hope. This is my comfort in my affliction, for Thy word hath quickened me.' [Psalm 119:49–50] And again he says in verse 76 – 'Let, I pray Thee, Thy merciful kindness be for my comfort, according to Thy word unto Thy servant.'

The 86th Psalm is a great mingling together of light and darkness. There are very deep things there. The soul is spoken of even as being delivered from the lowest hell, but God is equal to all the need. David asks to have his soul made to rejoice; and to whom does he look to do this? To God; and because he did, he found the help and comfort that he sought. 'But Thou, O Lord, art a God full of compassion, and gracious, long suffering, and plenteous in mercy and truth. O turn unto me, and have mercy upon me; give Thy strength unto Thy servant, and save the son of Thine handmaid. Show me a token for good, that they which hate me may see it and be ashamed, because Thou, Lord, hast holpen me and comforted me.'

When David was utterly perplexed, he said, 'In the multitude of my thoughts within me Thy comforts delight my soul;' [Psalm 94:19] and when the time of all times for comfort should come, then God as the God of all comfort would be at hand. 'Yea, though I walk through the valley of the shadow of death, I will fear no evil; for Thou art with me, Thy rod and Thy staff they comfort me.' [Psalm 23:4]

Now, let us look for a moment at the prophets; for it will be a grand help to us, if we have it firmly grafted in our minds that God Himself is the One to go to in our search after comfort.

Zion had sinned greatly against the Lord; and according to the usual rule of God's dealings, after the sin comes punishment. Zion ought never to have known 'waste places,' or a 'desert,' or a

[15]

'wilderness;' and certainly, considering what Jerusalem had done against God, He might naturally have been supposed to be the last quarter in which she could seek for any comfort. But the word which the Lord told the prophet to speak was a word after His fashion, and not after man's. 'For the Lord shall comfort Zion, He shall comfort all her waste places, and He shall make her wilderness like Eden, and her desert like the garden of the Lord; joy and gladness shall be found therein, thanksgiving and the voice of melody.' [Isa.51:3.] Observe how God is acting with the largeness which is becoming to Himself. Whenever there is great largeness of blessing, we may be sure that it is He that is at work. For His work has a fulness of blessing, like a number and variety of precious stones all set in the one ring, and given to the one person. This is God's way of comforting.

The angel of the Lord, in Zechariah chapter one, cried to God on behalf of Jerusalem, and said, 'O Lord of hosts, how long wilt Thou not have mercy on Jerusalem, and on the cities of Judah against which Thou hast had indignation these three score and ten years.' The angel does not hide the fact that the One he cried to is the One who had in righteous judgment permitted all the trouble. Yet from that very One comes the comfort: 'And the Lord answered the angel that talked with me with good words and comfortable words;' and here, as in the other case, comes the profusion of His mercy. 'Thus saith the Lord of hosts, I am returned to Jerusalem with mercies; My house shall be built in it, saith the Lord of hosts.' 'Thus saith the Lord of hosts, My cities through prosperity shall yet be spread abroad; and the Lord shall yet comfort Zion, and shall yet choose Jerusalem.'

Similarly in Jeremiah, He says of Himself, 'For I will turn their mourning into joy, and will comfort them.' [31:13.] 'And will speak comfortably unto her,' He says in Hosea 2:14. 'I am He that comforteth you,' He says in Isaiah 51:12. And in the day of thanksgiving – this is to be the song [Isa. 12:1] 'O Lord, I will praise Thee: though Thou wast angry with me, Thine anger is turned away, and Thou comfortedst me.' 'For the iniquity of his covetousness was I wroth and smote him. I hid Me and was wroth, and he went on frowardly in the way of his heart. I have seen his ways and will heal him. I will lead him also, and restore comforts unto him and to his mourners.' [Isa. 57:17, 18.]

Many of these texts will meet us again. I desire them now to be of use in this one blessed particular of bringing us nearer to God Himself. And these three things I set in the forefront of my little book.

(1) Get firmly convinced that God, God Himself, God the Father, the Father of our Lord Jesus Christ, and our Father, is a God of comfort. Read these many declarations which He has

given of Himself, over and over again, until you ingrain the idea into your hearts. Believe that comfort is a thing He thinks about, values, knows the need of to us.

(2) Do not look anywhere else for your prime and first comfort. I do not deny that there is much comfort in friends, in happy feelings, in books, in many of the surrounding circumstances which prove alleviations in illness; but I want you to gather in your thoughts, and feel that the only sure comfort is with God.

(3) Expect comfort from God. Man's expectation is generally a prelude to God's action. We must first open our mouth, and then he will fill it. We must fill the waterpots up to the brim, seeing that He is going to turn all this water into the good wine.

Let these texts put you into the proper attitude of expectation. Say 'Speak, Lord, for Thy servant heareth.' Let God know that there is somebody looking to Him for comfort, some poor child of His unsatisfied, and in want, and that it is you; and who knows but that even in the very pages of this little book He may give you all you need.

2: HINDRANCES TO OUR BELIEVING THAT GOD IS A GOD OF COMFORT

When the sun shines brightly its warm beams draw up the damp fogs from the earth, and they often obscure its lustre. When a lamp is lit, the brighter it shines, the more the insects that gather round it. And so the brighter any truth of God, the more does Satan endeavour to gather about it such mists as will obscure it, if indeed he cannot extinguish it altogether.

And so we may expect to find that there are many hindrances to a full belief that God is a God of comfort. I am not in any wise surprised that it should be so; and I would be instrumental by God's blessing in removing them. But before we can remove these hindrances, we must see them. And what are they?

One great hindrance is our sense of demerit – how very unworthy we are of comfort at all; and especially of such an One as God taking it in hand to comfort us. About that unworthiness there cannot be the shadow of a doubt. It is quite right that you should feel that you are not worthy of anything good from God at all. So far from finding fault with the feeling, it is a blessed one to start with; and if unhappily you had it not, I should have had to say, 'We cannot advance even the first step into God's comfort, until we get to see and believe this. For God will not have any man talk or think of merit.'

'Merit I have none to bring,
Only to Thy cross I cling.'

Those are the sentiments of such as are fit for
comfort, and are sure to get it.

So now, first of all: be very thankful that you
feel undeserving of any comfort, or anything
else that is good. That in itself should bring you
some comfort. For if you feel this, you have not to
go through all the humbling and teaching dealings
of God, by which He takes the pride out of people.
If you are already empty, God has not to empty
you. And let me tell you further that if you had
not felt so unworthy of comfort, there is no telling
what discipline you might not have had to go
through. You might have been made ten times
more uncomfortable than you are now. The law of
God as broken, and you as the breaker, might
have been shewn in such terrible colours as to
break you up altogether. You might have been
brought into deeper waters in the way of illness,
even than those in which you are now. I am glad
God has not to deal more heavily with you on that
point. 'He filleth the hungry with good things,
but the rich He sends empty away.' 'This poor
man cried unto the Lord, and the Lord delivered
him out of all his troubles.' 'I am no more worthy
to be called Thy son.' There was the sense of
demerit in the prodigal, and we know how
blessedly it ended with him. Well, if you are the
hungry man, and the poor man, and the prodigal

son, so you shall be filled, and delivered, and received.

There is something else which you will be sure to find hindering you from believing that God can possibly be a God of comfort to you.

You know that you have a depraved, suspicious nature. As soon as Adam fell, he became suspicious of God; and all his posterity have inherited this suspicion from him. Indeed, suspicion is a part of the temptation with which Eve was first assailed; for when Satan told her that God did know that in the day she and Adam ate of the tree, then their eyes should be opened, and they should be as gods knowing good and evil, what is this but infusing a suspicion into the woman's mind, that God grudged her this knowledge, and was afraid of her becoming like Himself.

This element of suspicion was strong in the first temptation, and it has continued strong ever since. Therefore, it is no wonder if you suspect God, and have hard thoughts of Him.

Now here is an evil, plain and well defined, against which we must fight. We must not be always suspecting God. If He says one thing to us, we must not think that He means another. We must not suppose that He is double-minded in any of His ways. We must say to ourselves, 'He said so and so, and therefore He means it, I will take Him at His word; I will not go about seeking to put two or three meanings on His plain declarations; what He says I will take in

[21]

the plain English of it.' We must not go about looking for double meanings, and limitations, and all sorts of things out of the common. The more we keep in the common road of speech and meaning with God the better.

Now, think of that, dear friend; and do not suspect God any more. It is partly because of this suspicion that we misunderstand God; and whereever there is misapprehension there is confusion and trouble.

There is one more hindrance out of many which I would mention; and that is, the old bad habit of not looking to Him for what is good.

This old, suspicious and misunderstanding nature of ours, used to make us think that God was the last person to whom we could look for what was good. If we wanted judgment, and anger for sin, and punishment, and suchlike things, then He was the quarter in which to look for it; but certainly not for good things. And yet when He revealed Himself to Moses, what do we read as His glory?

When the Israelites were under the Divine hand, suffering severely from God Himself for their sin, what, humanly speaking, could be more unlikely than that from God Himself should come their help? Yet see what is said in Deuteronomy 4:27–31: 'And the Lord shall scatter you among the nations; and ye shall be left few in number among the heathen, whither the Lord shall lead you. And there ye shall serve gods, the work of men's hands, wood and stone, which neither see, nor hear, nor eat, nor smell.'

Now, whence are they to find help? They are to look to *Him* for it. 'But if from thence thou shalt seek the Lord thy God, thou shalt find Him, if thou seek Him with all thy heart and with all thy soul. When thou art in tribulation, and all these things are come upon thee, even in the latter days, if thou turn to the Lord thy God, and shalt be obedient unto His voice (for the Lord thy God is a merciful God) He will not forsake thee, neither destroy thee, nor forget the covenant of thy fathers, which He sware unto them.' What God says as plainly as possible is this. You have offended against Me, but it is to Me you must look. 'O Israel, (said He in Hosea 13:9) thou hast destroyed thyself, but in Me is thy help.'

But perhaps you say, 'I never thought much of God, I never used to look to Him.' Well, that has been very bad in the past; but what we are concerned with is the present. The past is dead and gone, and let the dead bury their dead. We cannot alter the bad and foolish past. It will always remain what it was. But what we are concerned with is that it should not carry itself on into the present, that it should not hurt us now, that it should be indeed 'a past.'

Now, say to yourself: That is a bad old habit of mine, not looking to God. I must break with it altogether. Let Him now make all things new with me. This foolish and ungainful past has no right to put in a claim upon the present. Sufficient unto the day is the evil thereof.

Now, when difficulties arise they are very apt to discourage. That is their natural tendency. A discouraged man is always a weak man. This Satan knows very well; and therefore, he puts all sorts of discouragements in the way of our going to God for comfort.

If you find one reason after another rising up in your mind, why you should not look to God to comfort you, instead of being down-hearted, say, 'This is the most natural thing in the world, precisely what I might have expected. This is part of the bad old way which I am abandoning. I think Satan must see I am in earnest in looking to God, by his raising up so many obstacles in my path.'

I have no doubt, my friend, that you have a great many discouragements. Was ever anything great and abiding brought about without them? They are the very atmosphere in which what is great, and good, and enduring, is perfected.

Draw courage from discouragement. Say, 'Satan sees I am on the right road now, and is trying to hinder me all he can. Strait is my gate, and narrow is my way; and that is a good sign that the end of that way is right.'

You must not simply condemn yourself. You have done that once – let it be once and for all. If you spend all your time in condemning yourself, you will have none to spend in finding God. I do not believe that God is well pleased with a man's spending all his time in self-condemnation. He wills him to live in the spirit of self-condemnation: how indeed can he live in anything else? But to be always moaning and condemning himself, I cannot think is what He wills as His people's lot. I think God might well say to us, 'What! all looking at self, and never a look at Me! What! look at Me, and never a bit of comfort out of it! Are your sins of more importance than My grace? are they to occupy all the ground, and no room to be left for Me to act in comfort and blessing, the way in which I love to act?' Be sure of this, something more than your sins must be manifested, if God is to be glorified. He will be more glorified by your being comforted than by your continually refusing to be comforted, or crying out that you are unworthy to be comforted. Self-condemnation is very good in its place, but it is very bad out of its place; and it is out of its place, when we make it so big that it can blot out the comfort of God. We may put a penny piece so close to our eyes as to hide out the sun itself; and we may put our little selves into such a position as to blot out God.

Moreover, you must not give up in this matter of comfort, or in any point of the divine life, because you do not seem to get on. Often we are getting on, when we do not know that we are. God never changes, nor are His mercies dependent upon our 'getting on.' This is a measuring of ourselves by ourselves, and such is not the measure of the Lord.

Nor must you give way to low and desponding thoughts because you do not experience any spiritual ecstasies. There are many children of God, who have never known anything approaching to spiritual ecstasy at all, nor attained to anything beyond a calm and peaceful trust in Him. They lay still on their beds in peace. They believed in a glory to be revealed. They believed in a future, and were content to wait for it. Ecstasies might be very bad for us here. Some of the most favoured servants of God, and most consistent Christians, never had any ecstasy in their lives. And some who had gone up very high in ecstasies, have gone down very low in despondencies.

Do not court ecstasies. Do not look upon them as signs. Do not consider them in any way as essential to the Christian life, or the comfort thereof. If God give them, it needs that He give grace with them; and who knows but that it needs that He give discipline too.

Paul was caught up into the third heaven, and heard words which it was not lawful to utter; and to make that ecstasy safe, he had to receive a thorn in the flesh, which, though he prayed thrice for its removal, was not taken away.

Lay your account for being a hindered man; and when clouds come between you and God, often say 'Ah, that is a hindrance. It does not change God, it does not change my position toward God; but it is a hindrance, and is doing a hinderer's work.'

And when the hindrances come, let them not daunt us. Let us say, 'These are what we are to expect, but they have no power as against the Lord.' Millions of hindered men have passed out of their clouds and sorrows. Millions have entered the land where there are hindrances no more. How could I expect that Satan would allow me to have any good thing unmolested? I must carry on the Christian warfare on my bed, the same as if I were in the world. Sooner or later I too shall have my full triumph; and shall shout 'Thanks be to God, which giveth me the victory through my Lord Jesus Christ.'

3: HELPS TO OUR BELIEVING
THAT GOD IS A GOD OF COMFORT

It would be a poor comfort to point out the existence of hindrances unless we believed that they could be overcome, and also could show how this might be done.

'Alas!' the poor tried man might say, 'I know my hindrances only too well; help me to put them out of the way, and then you will confer on me a favour indeed.'

This is what I should like now to do. This is a fitting part of a Comfort Book.

Now, one of the most effectual ways of getting rid of these hindrances is to track them out, and ascertain whence they come.

I have no doubt many of them come from certain depraved thinkings about God; and consequently, the helps should come from thinkings also, only of the right kind. We must keep close to thoughts of God. We must meet Satan's dark thoughts and suggestions about God with bright thoughts about Him. For if we do not, he will always be able to bring God up terribly against us. However we may divert our minds, the evil one will always keep saying, 'But ah, what about God? All is not right with Him; and what is more, all never can be.'

But if we have gone to God, and have well-assured thoughts of Him, then God can never come before us as a dark shadow, but as light.

We shall know Him as a Father indeed; and if Satan come to vex us with thoughts about Him, we shall say, 'We know who He is – our Father who is in heaven.'

I consider then God's character as my great help to believing Him to be a God of comfort.

And first of all, from the mere fact of His being generous, we may judge that He is very likely to be a God of comfort.

Everywhere in Scripture He is represented to us as a large-hearted God. He is One that hath no pleasure in the death of a sinner, but would rather that he turned from his iniquity and lived. He says, 'Open thy mouth wide and I will fill it'; 'the sins and iniquities of My people I will remember no more.' How much more generous God is than man, we have remarkably set before us in what He says to the prophet Jeremiah – 'Hast thou seen what backsliding Israel hath done? she is gone up upon every high mountain, and under every green tree, and there hath played the harlot. And I said after she had done all these things, Turn thou unto Me' [3:6–7].

Others would have said, 'Begone,' but God said, 'Return.' That was generosity indeed. In the first verse of this chapter God shows that man's way of treating a person under similar circumstances would be very different; but then He is God and not man; and His ways and thoughts are not like our ways and thoughts; His generosity is altogether beyond ours.

Happening to open the Concordance this moment, I came upon five texts one after another where God is spoken of as being intreated with success. 'After that, God was intreated for the land:' [2 Sam 21:14]. 'The Lord was intreated for the land, and the plague was stayed:' [2 Sam. 24:25]. 'They cried and He was intreated of them:' [1 Chron. 5:20]. 'Manasseh prayed and God was intreated of him:' [2 Chron. 33:13]. 'We besought God and He was intreated of us:' [Ezra 8:23]. God is 'long-suffering, plenteous in goodness and mercy.' And in the parable of the prodigal son, generous dealing is shown to the very full; the father receives the wretched sinner just as he is; and reproaching him not, restores him to favour, and clothes him in the best robe, and kills for him the fatted calf.

Now, if I want anything, it is a great encouragement to me in going to ask for it that I know I have to deal with a generous person. I feel he will be predisposed to help me, and to deal liberally with me, and to do me good. And let this thought comfort you. There is not one niggard word about God in all the Bible. You will be sure to get from Him, simply because He is what He is, whatever He has promised to bestow.

And if God be generous, then He will be self-communicative, that is, He will be always outputting good. God is not content with simply having His goodness, and keeping it to Himself.

He spared not His only Son, but freely gave Him up for us all; and how shall He not with Him also freely give us all things?

If we had to go to a person for anything, who is actually wanting to give away the very things we needed, what wonderful spirit it would put into us to go to him for what we required.

Now, can God have all that would make us happy and comfortable, and bestow never a taste on us? Certainly not! Therefore, if you want, He will communicate Himself to you; and what He communicates must be Himself, must be like Himself, and therefore it must be good; it will be the giving of Himself to you as you are, and with your particular want. He will pour His streams into all your hollow places, all your dry wells, and on your parched lands, and empty water-courses; where you are driest and most in want is the place where He will most surely come.

Then, we may take great comfort from considering that God stands to us in the relation of a Father; and forasmuch as He must from His very nature do everything in the best and most perfect manner, and to the fullest extent also, we may be sure He will be to us better than ever any earthly father has been to a son.

If any of us who are old, and have experienced the trials and struggles of life, were told that our father had risen from his grave with a thousand-fold more love than he ever had to us when he was alive, and with plenty of wealth wherewith practically to show that love, and with wisdom which would effectually prevent his making any mistake, we should have wonderful comfort indeed, no matter what immediate trial were pressing on us.

But we have something better. We have a Father in heaven; and He will not come short in the fulfilment of even one of the functions of a parent.

Comfort yourself, then, with the thought that the One with whom you have to do is in every way One whose very relationship to you secures your getting what you want. If your Father will not comfort you, who will? He is the most likely person to get comfort from; therefore the proper person to go to for it.

And because He is a Father you may expect all tender comfort. It is through the tender mercy of our God that the dayspring from on high hath visited us. James tells us that 'the Lord is pitiful and of tender mercy.' [1:11] The injunction to be kind one to another, to be tender-hearted, and to forgive one another, is all grounded on such things in God – 'even as God for Christ's sake hath forgiven you' [Eph. 4:32].

Now, if instead of thus looking at God and at all that is to well forth from Him because He is what He is, we look at ourselves, and at all that we deserve, we shall have no comfort at all. Comfort will never travel to us by this latter path. We are to look at ourselves, expecting to find all emptiness, and not wanting to make the matter one whit better than it is. We must not be surprised or startled or down-hearted at realizing this emptiness; it simply arises from our being what we are. If we set about making discoveries concerning ourselves, they will be all in the line of this emptiness; more and more of it, the more we look.

But all the discoveries of God will be of fulness; and in putting the two together must lie our comfort.

Bathe your thoughts then in God. Be rich in God – poor in yourselves, but rich in Him.

You see what He is. All His nature, all His sayings, all His doings argue comfort. Not comfort for the impenitent and the independent, and for those who think they have no need; but for all who wish to be humble, and in want, and to be supplied from a source outside themselves.

Say then thus, in your communings with yourselves: –

Who knows so well what God is as Himself? and all that He has told me leads comfortwards. I will not give God a bad character by expecting only gloom from Him.

I will not take Satan's opinion about God; what interest can he have but to malign Him?

I will not take my own deceitful, and suspicious, and ignorant heart's surmisings about Him; for from my poor fallen nature they are sure to be warped.

I will throw myself upon God, as He has revealed Himself. I will keep my eyes fixed on Him; and I will shut them to all else.

I will keep to what He has revealed. I can only be what I am – empty; and He can only be what He is – the Supplier of that emptiness. Out of His fulness then shall I receive; and because He is what He is, I shall have grace to help in every time of need.

4: A COMFORT IN PAIN

We must not undervalue pain. It is a folly to say that we should be above being moved by it – that, as it is only for a time, we ought not to make anything of it.

To get comfort in my time of pain, I take up altogether a different line of thought. So far from making nothing of pain, I make a great deal of it. I believe it to be a very real trouble, a very great trial, something which makes a great demand upon my faith and patience, and all my powers of body and mind too. I consider it an insult to any one suffering pain to make light of his suffering. I do not consider that he is a Spartan who glories in bearing pain without sympathy. Nor am I one either. On the other hand, I like to feel for another's pain. I should be sorry if, when I saw a man or woman in suffering, I did not feel something.

Pain is an undeniable fact, and to try to do away with it is simply folly.

And hence comes part of my comfort. Be persuaded, then, that God does not make light of your pain. I am comforted in my suffering in the thought that God knows all about it, and feels for it too. Sympathy is a great balm; and you have the sympathy of God.

Then, why does He not remove your pain when He undoubtedly could do so by even one single word? Perhaps, you have sometimes had a hard thought about God on that account. You know that your physician, your friend who comes to see you and who sympathizes with you, would certainly remove your pain in one moment, if he could; and whereas God can, but does not, is His sympathy less than your friend's?

Certainly not! We do not see the reasons for pain; we are like children, who for a present advantage would forego any amount of future good; but our sympathizing Father is wise, with a full far-seeing wisdom; and He means us to get great blessing, if only we are willing that He should bless us in His own way.

Therefore, be comforted in every pain with the thought that it has not escaped the observation of God; but has been noted by Him, has been felt for by Him. 'My groaning is not hid from Thee.' [Psalm 38:9]. Pain is no vulgar thing when we bring it into connection with the sympathy of God.

Then, we come to the thought that Jesus suffered pain. Put that down as a second comfort; put it down as a great comfort. Christ (God and man) in His human nature, made of nerves and flesh and blood, just like yours, every nerve the same, every muscle the same, actually felt great pain; probably greater than any you have ever felt. A sharp pain was sharp, a dull grinding pain was dull and grinding to Him, just as such pains are with you. No doubt you have no pain but that He felt one like it, probably that very pain in its highest form upon the cross.

I think it will help you to bear your pain, and will comfort you in it, if you come into fellowship with Christ in regard to it. It is not the most heroic, the most excellent way, to shut yourself up, and bear it grimly alone. Perhaps, your nearest and dearest friends about you cannot enter into your sufferings; and that is sometimes likely to distress and irritate you; well, remember there is a friend who can — who in all our afflictions was afflicted; and that friend is in sympathy with you; and you are not unnoticed, and your pain is not under-valued. Surely, there is no small comfort here.

Another comfort in pain is the thought that all this shall have an end.

There is a prospect before you. Jesus, for the joy that was set before Him endured the cross, despising the shame. Every pain borne, is one pain less to bear.

And God would have us think of the end. He sets all the future blessedness before us, telling us of it before we attain to it, in order that it may cheer and encourage us on our way. Read what it says in Revelation 21:4: 'And God shall wipe away all tears from their eyes; and there shall be no more death, neither sorrow, nor crying, neither shall there be any more pain; for the former things are passed away.' I do not say that this makes the pain itself one whit less, but it gives us courage to bear it; it inspires us with hope in it; it gives us a glimpse of the final way out of it; and, to say the least, it cheers us.

Then, it is a comfort in painful illnesses that we are in fellowship with great ones. A vast number of God's most eminent servants have been pain-bearers. Many of these have had pains which no one knew anything of until they died; then, in their diaries, an account of their sufferings has been found.

And it is a comfort that pain is working blessing. 'No chastening is for the present joyous but grievous, but in the end it worketh the peaceable fruit of righteousness.' [Heb. 12:11.] Wasted labour is the worst of toil. To be trying to teach those who either cannot, or will not learn; to be tilling ground which has no heart, and can yield no adequate return; this, and all kindred work is double toil. And aimless pain is of this nature. But no pain is aimless, if only we will see that it has a design. God means it to work blessing. He means that it should leave something behind it. Pain has its place in the plan of our life, ever since the fall.

Then, why do not all men have it?

Because the plan of all men's lives is not the same; enough for us that if it come to us, it is in the plan of ours; and we must believe that it has not been put there for naught, but that God's good is coming our way; and to know that good is before us, is comfort in itself.

Note one comfort more. In pain, if properly borne, God can be pleased. But perhaps our pain may be so sharp, or may have worn us down so much that we cannot get the mind to work actively; we cannot have the idea of pleasing God strong before us.

Under these circumstances it is a comfort to think that God does not require us to think. He is no hard taskmaster. He only wills us to resign ourselves into His hands. We may do that, and lean back in our chairs, or on our pillows, and feel that we are pleasing Him, though we can have no active thoughts about Him.

So pain, bad as undoubtedly it is, is not altogether so comfortless a condition as we unthoughtfully or petulantly might suppose. It has comforts belonging to it which are its own; and, no doubt, some which are not elsewhere to be had.

'Whom the Lord loveth He chasteneth, and scourgeth every son that He receiveth;' and many an one can say: 'Before I was afflicted I went astray, but now have I kept Thy word.' [Psalm 119:67.]

Therefore let the one who suffers pain say these things to himself: —

'Thou, O my Saviour, didst suffer pain in the days of Thy flesh; shall the servant be above his Master? the disciple above his Lord?

'O my Saviour, Thou understandest my sufferings. I thank Thee that in Thy exaltation Thou feelest for me. I comfort myself in the sweet condescension and sympathy of Thy love.

'Touching this my pain, these things have an end. Open unto me, O my Lord, the vision of the blest; bring vividly to my heart the time when suffering shall be no more. Let heaven come before my weary eyes; and let me endure as seeing Thee, the invisible One, and the world invisible too. Let the painless eternity build up my strength in these my painful hours.

'I praise Thee, O my God, that I am in fellowship with the great ones of Thy kingdom in this my pain; and thus far in the communion of saints. O let me not disgrace that noble company! Strengthen me, O my God, by the remembrance of all they so nobly endured, and let me feel that I am not alone. Let a sense of fellowship make me strong.

'Let me not hinder Thy blessing, O my Father, by rejecting the means through which Thou sendest it. Let me not close up any of the avenues of Thy mercies. Let me expect that Thou wilt do me good. Consecrate my pain to Thy high uses. Sanctify it, that it may be a wealth-bringer unto me.

'Show me, O Lord, the light of Thy countenance in my pain, that I may know that Thou art pleased. Let me use my pain as an instrument wherewith to please Thee. Let me hear Thee speak unto me, and say that Thou acceptest this sacrifice at my hands.'

Thus, in the sympathies of Christ,

Thus, enduring that which has an end,

Thus, in the fellowship with great ones of the kingdom,

Thus, bearing that which brings blessing,

Thus, pleasing God,

Be comforted, suffering one, in thy pain. God has ordained no place to be wholly comfortless; and there are many comforts for thee here.

5. A COMFORT AS TO OUR BEING USELESS

There are few more distressing feelings than that of thinking ourselves useless. We feel melancholy at the thought, and almost degraded. We think we are a burden to others, we certainly become such to ourselves.

This idea is very likely to take possession of the mind of a sick person; and the more active the life in health, the more useless does one seem to oneself to be, when laid upon a bed of illness.

And here let me remind my readers that this Comfort book is not intended only for people who are in bed. Many of the most pitiable forms of illness and suffering will be found not on beds at all, but on sofas, in arm-chairs. Yes! many of the sick ones who may claim this book as their own are even walking about, but they are hit sore, and can do nothing that looks worth much.

I am free to confess at once that there is much that is very sad in such cases, much to depress, much to warp and sour the mind, much to make a sick man pass wrong judgment upon himself.

It is quite natural that when we see the train of daily life rolling off, we should feel sad at being left behind; that it should increase our sadness if we reflect that so has it been for many a long day; and perhaps so will it be for many a long day more; it may be, even to the end.

The nobler one's nature is, the more will one

feel this. To many, the feeling has been at times intolerable. Very often it has set up irritation and sin. It has warped the mind into such a morbid condition that it could not look calmly at the situation, and see under the surface, and get the comfort which undeniably is there.

It would indeed be dreadful and degrading to be utterly useless. It would add a fresh trial to those which already belong to the sick man. If he were indeed useless he must be very wretched, because he would be in violation of God's express intention, and of the whole plan of His providence; for in His whole creation there is not a single useless thing.

Now, here I think we shall find our first comfort. The good God, who has sent you your sickness, is the One who has ordained that nothing shall be useless. God has made you, and put you in your present position; and He meant you to be useful in it, of importance in it too.

You are certainly not ordained to be an exception to all creation; if you are, you must be a very strange person indeed; in fact, quite a curiosity in your way.

Now, I am sure you do not want to make out that you are unique in creation – the only specimen of a useless thing that the Almighty ever made. Why, that such an idea should be absurd is quite a comfort in itself.

Perhaps you think that all the juice is gone out of you, and that you are no better now than a dry bone, such as one of those seen by Ezekiel in the vision of the valley of dry bones; and concerning which the question is asked, 'Son of man, can these bones live?'

Well, let us take up for a moment this matter of the bone. Go to any London dust heap, and you will find sorters picking out from it carefully every bone. No doubt the people who ate the meat off them considered them done with, and threw them away; just as you consider yourself done for, and thrown on one side. But the bone has not come to its end yet. It is sent off to the boiling house, and there every portion of fat or gelatine that it can yield is extracted from it. The former goes to the soap maker, the latter is turned to account for the patent gelatine packets now in use for a score of different purposes. The turners get hold of those of any size, and convert them into thousands of fancy articles. Even the very small scraps are of use. Ground very fine and treated with sulphuric acid, they make the celebrated superphosphate manure, one of the best known fertilizers. Another very important product extracted from bones is phosphorus, an important part of the brain and nervous system, one of the substances which give light to the match. 'What diverse forms of new life await the old bone, as the rag picker recovers it from the dust heap! Its substance in the form of handles of knives, chessmen, paper knives, and so on, mingles with the everyday concerns of life – its hard work, and its enjoyments, and intellectual amusements – whilst in its fluid and manurial products yet more astonishing changes attend it, the moment it falls into the hands of the manufacturer. The difficulty that we feel in dealing with this seeming rubbish that we kick out of the way with our foot, is to follow it out into the many diverse forms it assumes upon its resurrection.'

How much better are you, my friend, than any bone, how much better than any *thing*! You are not a *thing*, but a man, or woman, one whom God made for His own glory; and concerning whom He did not change His purpose when He sent you illness. No, He only altered the sphere and method of your service and usefulness, promoting you, perhaps, to a much higher one than you had before. Remember that, if you are useless, it must be only by your own deliberate act; and you must not consider that it is the doing of God. God has not taken away all opportunities of usefulness from you by setting you in a useless place.

This is our first comfort here. The position is not by any means so bad, as at first sight it appeared. Cheer up; God has a place for you. God has something for you to do, and to be, in His kingdom. You are no poor trodden down creature; you have a place and a name before God.

It will help you very much to see this, if you remember that seeming uselessness is very different from real; and if you will determine to look below the surface, and to look at things in relation to God. Sometimes, we must look at things in relation to God and man; and sometimes to God alone.

That the bone has lost its usefulness is not true. It has great uses, if only they are brought out by proper treatment. It has fulfilled all its functions, in being during life part of an animal; and now it has a new set of functions to enter on.

And all your uselessness is only in appearance. True! you cannot take part in the business of life (no more can this bone in the motion of any animal), but you can be useful in other ways. Your patience, your resignation, your glorifying God in the fires, your word of good to others, all are useful, inestimably precious in the sphere of His kingdom in which He has now appointed you to act.

Sick man, you have a place of usefulness for God, not the old place, but His place – the place which is best in the eyes of the all-wise One.

Sometimes, in talking to sick people, I put it in this way: In a great army going forth to battle there is the artillery with its wagons, and guns, and teams and mounted artillery-men. It makes a great show – no one can fail to be impressed with the thunder of its guns, and with the execution they do. Perhaps, we would think it a fine thing to belong to the artillery. Then come the cavalry – a brave show the regiments make as they charge the enemy; and we would think it a

fine thing to be mounted on one of those splendid
chargers – the uniform is striking; if we wanted
to fight for our country, we should be well
pleased to be in that branch of the service. But
who are these in sombre uniforms of dark green?
– a scattered band, stealing along quietly – one
mounting a tree, hiding in its foliage; another
crouching in the corn; a third sheltering behind
a stump; a fourth and fifth lying flat on their
face and hands. Are these cowards, skulking in
the day of battle? Are they men who, whatever
brings them here, do not belong to the king's army
at all? No – their button bears the 'crown' – these
are 'the rifles.' They form a brigade of their own;
and this is the way they fight when occasion so
requires. That sombre uniform is essential to the
work these men have to do. They are lying in
wait to pick off the officers on the enemy's side.
They may have to wait silently, patiently, and
unseen, for a long time; but they are taking part
in the battle, just as much as those who come
out more prominently. And when the victory is
won, and the rewards are given, these men will
wear a medal on their breasts just as others, and
will be accounted as having taken part in the
battle, and contributed to the victory, just as much
as they.

In 1 Samuel chapter 30:21–25, you read of
two hundred men who were so faint that they
could not follow David, 'whom they had made
also to abide at the brook Besor: and they went

forth to meet David, and to meet the people that were with him. and when David came near to the people he saluted them. Then answered all the wicked men and men of Belial, of those that went with David, and said, "Because they went not with us, we will not give them aught of the spoil that we have recovered, save to every man his wife and his children, that they may lead them away, and depart." Then said David, "Ye shall not do so, my brethren, with that which the Lord hath given us, who hath preserved us, and delivered the company that came against us into our hand. For who will hearken unto you in this matter? but as his part is that goeth down to the battle, so shall his part be that tarrieth by the stuff: they shall part alike." And it was so, from that day forward, that he made a statute and an ordinance for Israel unto this day.'

The men who are keeping garrison are just as important in the war, looking at it as a whole, as those who go out and take the field. If there were not garrisons in such and such fortified places, the troops in the field would have no base for their operations – nothing to fall back upon – and perhaps, the war could not be carried on at all.

God's plans, His work, His kingdom are a great whole; and though you would be useless, and worse than useless here, and there, as a rifle-man would be if he got in amongst the cavalry or artillery, yet in your own place you are of the greatest use. God has a use for you, though man cannot see it; though perhaps, you cannot see it yourself. All you have to do is to say, 'Am I in the place where God has put me?' and if you feel that you are, then, depend upon it, the all-wise God would not do so foolish a thing as to put you where you could be of no use.

Let me tell you another little similitude by which I try to comfort sick people.

Here is a lady with a bag of beautiful wools of all colours. Her little boy comes to her while she is at work and says, 'Oh, mother, what beautiful colours – red, blue, pink, green; I like them all; they will look pretty in your picture when it is finished. But here is a skein of black. I don't like that; it is a nasty dull colour: and there is only one skein of it. That cannot do any good. I will take it away, for it is only spoiling the look of these pretty wools.'

'No, no, my child,' says the mother, 'that is a very precious skein, you must not touch it; I will shew you by and by how useful it is.'

So the work goes on, and is almost finished, when the mother shews it to the child. But the latter, instead of exclaiming how much he admires it, looks at it in astonishment, and says, 'Why, mother, the men, and women, and children, and horses, and dogs have no eyes; they look as if they were not real at all.'

Then the mother produces her skein of black wool, and in a few minutes works in the eyes; and then the whole thing looks life-like, and now the child has learned the use of the skein of black.

And thus is it with us. Our illness is to us the skein of black that makes our particular life a useful one, that makes us fill up the place where black is needed in the great plan of God. We, perhaps, are the shadows in God's great picture. And what picture could be drawn with nothing but light – what picture, I mean, which concerns earth? The great picture of God's love, so far as earth is concerned, is shaded heavily with the shadow of the Cross. So that, as far as being useless is concerned, you may be greatly comforted. Unless it is your deliberate wish to be so, you neither are, nor can be useless.

Perhaps, in your illness, you are being promoted in the kingdom of God. When that bone of which we were speaking a little time ago, was ground up and changed into superphosphate of lime, how subtle did it become in its influence! It then had power to enter into the minute hair-like roots and fibres of plants, it could combine with the elements; it could do wonders. Crushed corn makes bread, trodden grapes make wine, pressed olives yield oil, the frankincense that feels the fire, floats upwards in perfumed wreaths toward the sky. The corn of wheat abiding alone is not fruitful; it is when it dies that it enters into the harvest ranks; the branch that bears fruit is pruned that it may bring forth more fruit.

So then, sick man or woman, do not mope and be downcast; consider yourself not to be useless.

If you are sufficiently free from pain, and have sufficient strength, find out some occupation for yourself. It will be especially helpful to you if that occupation has to do with the relief of some one else in sickness. If your means are small and your occupation will bring you in something, what you get thus will be doubly sweet. But propose to yourself some aim, some work. While preparing this page for the press the following reached me in a letter.

'Elizabeth lives at a little village called K——. When eighteen years old she was working in a mine, and met with a terrible accident, getting her spine broken in *three* places, and *five* ribs broken also – two on one side, three on the other. She has now lived on in this state *forty-five* years, without any feeling below her waist, and one leg bent completely under her.

'She was one of a large family, all of whom have died but one sister, an old woman of over seventy, who lives with her and takes care of her. The said sister is *deaf and dumb*, and cannot read: her name is Abigail. It is wonderful to see the two together – so fond of each other. Elizabeth has no power to move herself in her bed; she is turned from her back to her chest by Abigail, who understands a little by means of signs.

'Notwithstanding her terrible affliction, Elizabeth is the brightest Christian I have seen. She is full of rejoicing and gratitude, and remarked the other day to a lady who went in, "How good it is of the Lord to let the sun shine in at my little window!" She is so great a favourite with the neighbours, (and no wonder, always thinking of others) that a poor woman who was dying and leaving a baby a few weeks old, would not be satisfied until Elizabeth promised to take it and bring it up. This she actually did, and the child lived to be fourteen, when it died of consumption, very happy.

'Another little instance of the way she is always ready to help others: a lady going in one morning, found her lying as usual on her chest, but with her hands stretched out of the bed, busily kneading dough to make a loaf for a family in want near her.'

Under any circumstances you may be of great use by being contented and cheerful in your trouble. Those around you will see that God sustains you, and will bless Him and glorify Him, and perhaps learn to trust Him too.

Here is another account of a useful Christian which I also received while engaged on these pages.

'You asked me to send you a short account of Elizabeth, the poor young woman whom we knew at B——, where my father was living for some years. She lay for eighteen years on her back, not able even to be moved on her side; but notwithstanding this, she was one of the happiest people I have ever seen. It was a pretty little cottage in the grounds, close to the water's edge, that she lived in; but she could see nothing of the beauty around her (of which she used to be so fond) except in a high tide, when she used greatly to enjoy the sight of the boats as they passed. She had slipped on the rocks when a girl of sixteen, falling on her back, gradually lost the use of her limbs, and soon was unable to be moved from her bed. Often she suffered great pain, and hardly ever slept more than one hour, or two hours at longest, in the night. Yet a brighter, happier face it was impossible to see, or a more wonderful example of "rejoicing in tribulation." She used often to say, "This has been a blessed sickness to me, and nothing *less* would have done, I'm sure." Naturally very full of life and spirits, it seemed all the more wonderful, her extraordinary patience.

'My mother used always to say, she was a blessing to the whole neighbourhood; some of the roughest men used to come and sit by her bedside and take a "word" from Elizabeth, and a little book (of which she always kept a stock); whoever was in trouble invariably confided in her, and her *great* sympathy in others' sorrows made people forget she had any of her own!

'She used to say that her long nights gave her time to pray about all the troubles that were told to her. Some days, when feeling a little better, she would knit, or read and write for a short time, but not very often. She was given a water-bed the last few years of her life, for which she never ceased to thank God; and the *smallest* kindness was always so gratefully received, that everyone felt it a pleasure to do anything for her. She would also "rejoice with those who rejoiced" in a very beautiful way.

'She died about three years ago, praising God to the last, although for several months in great suffering and saying, "she would willingly bear it all over again for the comfort and joy she had felt in her Lord." '

It would, however, be beside the purpose of this little book to enter at any length upon this subject. This is a comfort book; and apart from all such considerations as these, I hope, I have said enough to give you some comfort on the subject of not being useless.

We must not think so meanly of ourselves as to suppose that God does not think us worth anything, and that we are thrown aside as something worthless. We may think meanly of ourselves in a bad, as well as in a good way. As a man thinks of himself, so, often, will he be. There is a motto belonging to a certain noble family – *Noblesse oblige* – Nobility obliges – that is, 'I am a nobleman, therefore I must act like a nobleman.' Feel that you are useful in God's kingdom, and you will feel the desire to act as though you were.

And then a whole cloud of miserable and depressing thoughts will be dispelled; and you will feel strengthened and revived. God wills that

you should be somebody still, and you will feel
that you are somebody; and that you have your
place on earth now, and will have it in heaven
hereafter.

6: A COMFORT IN FELT UNWORTHINESS

When we are sick, we are often much troubled by a deep consciousness of our unworthiness. We see ourselves to be very bad – much worse than we used to think ourselves to be; and this depresses us very much. We get low about ourselves spiritually.

We have now more time to think. Many things become stripped of the false colours they wore, of the excuses which we made for them; we see them as they are, and ourselves as having been guilty of them; and we become very downcast.

Now this is not to be a comfortless state. No state but that of living in impenitence and sin, and away from God, is to be absolutely comfortless. And that is not your state. So far from its being your state, nothing troubles you so much as sin, and your having been a sinner, and your being one now; and this is a state which God accounts a suitable one for giving comfort in. The more unworthy that comfort in yourself, the more likely to be comforted by God!

Rejoice, sick one, in feeling unworthy.

Thank God for feeling unworthy.

Expect blessing and comfort, as belonging to realized unworthiness.

Think, first of all, that this is the very thing God wants you to feel. Never a child has He had, but that He taught him this. He made Job say, 'I abhor myself, and repent in dust and ashes.' [42:6]. He brought Ezra on his knees to say, 'O my God, I am ashamed and blush to lift up my face to Thee, my God, for our iniquities are increased over our head, and our trespass is grown up into the heavens' [Ezra 9:6.] He makes the holy Daniel say, 'O Lord, righteousness belongeth unto Thee, but unto us confusion of faces as at this day' [Dan. 9:7]. Jacob said, 'I am not worthy of the least of all the mercies and of all the truth which Thou hast shewed unto Thy servant' [Gen. 32:10]. The prodigal son said that he was no more worthy to be called his father's son [Luke 15:19]. As for David, the Psalms are full of realizations of his unworthiness; and if there were no other confessions of it, the 51st Psalm alone would be enough.

You are therefore in the company of David, and Job, and Ezra, and Daniel, and Jeremiah, and Isaiah, and Hosea; and, indeed, all the saints of God with whom he has dealt by the Spirit. The path of realized unworthiness must be the right one for you to tread, when it was trodden by all these holy men.

Do not then make yourself uncomfortable because you are feeling unworthy. That is the best thing to feel – remember, it is what God wants you to feel. You are now in God's way; do not want to feel anything different from what you do; you are just right; the farther you travel on this road the better. Surely, to be certain of being in the right way is a great comfort in itself.

This is a feeling according to truth. Wherever there is the truth, there is health and soundness; and the thing will work out well. What you are in search of is truth as regards your soul's health and soul's affairs; and you may be sure you have it here. Do not meddle with the feeling. Do not want to twist or change it. Do not allow a voice to say to you, 'Oh! you would be ever so much more comfortable, if you could only feel yourself somewhat worthy; or, if you could do something to make yourself a little worthy.' That is all a mistake. You would thus immediately get into a region of falsehood; and the lie would raise up God against you, whereas now He is for you. And the lie would begin to work out all sorts of evils, for God resisteth the proud. It is the hungry that He fills with good things; but you would then no longer be the hungry, but the rich man; and we know what happens to him, he is sent empty away. Say, 'I feel and know I am unworthy; and I mean to hold fast to this feeling; I wish it to grow more and more; I wish to die in this feeling; I wish to appear before God in it; I wish to feel it throughout all eternity.'

Another comfort which you are to take to yourself from this feeling of unworthiness has already been suggested by that text, 'He hath filled the hungry with good things, but the rich He hath sent empty away.' This comfort is, that when unworthiness is felt, it gives room for blessing. God will not pour anything good into a false measure, or into that which cannot hold it, or into that in which there is no room for it.

Now, are not you in just the right condition for mercy? You are saying, and feeling too, before God (and the whole point of the matter consists in the feeling), 'Alas, I am dreadfully bad; I am a guilty creature, and a mean one, and I have nothing to offer Him;' and we know how God replies to such a man – 'He is empty; then there is room for Me, and Mine – I will fill him.'

Yes, there is plenty of room in you now for Christ. Christ will fill you with Himself; and when the Father sees the Son in you – all the Son – His own beloved Son, and not a bit of your own poor fallen self, and your own poor perishing things, He will be well pleased.

And so, you may sit in your arm-chair, or lie back upon your pillow a comforted man – all unworthy in yourself, but all worthy in Christ; having exactly what God wants to see in you, so that you know He must be well pleased.

It would be miserable indeed, if we had to stop at our own unworthiness. But to know that, is only just a means to an end; we have not to tarry in such a disagreeable state; we are to go on – on – and then rejoice, and to feel, and to say, and to sing, 'I am worthy in Christ. Yes, I myself am worthy in Him; God looks at me in Him, and counts me worthy in Him; I have worthiness

– plenty of worthiness – God's own worthiness – enough for the judgment – enough for heaven; all Christ's, but also all mine!'

And now, be comforted also in the thought that you are spared you know not how much chastisement, how much hard dealing, how much pulling down; because sooner or later, if you are to be saved, the lesson of unworthiness must be learned. It may be that you have much yet to learn on this subject. Indeed, we may be sure that, if we are the Lord's, we shall be learning ever more and more our own unworthiness.

But do not be discouraged at this. There is great comfort for you here also. You shall never learn anything bad about yourself, without learning something correspondingly good about Christ. You are none the worse, really, for finding out that you are worse than you thought. It is only that more light has come into your heart; and you see more than you did before. Things are really no worse, only you know more about them. God knows a great deal more about you, than you will ever know about yourself; and He has made provision according to His knowledge.

Therefore, when you find out a new thing about your bad heart, or bad life, let your first thought be, 'That is provided for in Christ.'

Humble yourself – the lower the better; but always, with Christ before you.

Humility without Christ will make you weak; with Him, it will make you strong. Our own unworthiness would crush us, unless it went hand in hand with the worthiness in Him.

And so, take to yourself that comfort which your most gracious God and kind Father has provided for you, and in that, be at peace.

7: A COMFORT TO COUNTER ENVIOUS THOUGHTS ABOUT OTHERS

Every condition in life has its own peculiar trials and temptations. Sometimes the same trials and temptations, as to kind, visit us in each of these conditions; but they have certain differences in their way of attack, which make them suit the exact condition in which we are.

To adapt, is a proof of wisdom and skill; and this is precisely what Satan does.

The time of illness has its own particular class of temptations; and they are all so nicely adapted to our circumstances that a long wearing illness will often require a different kind of temptation from that which belongs to a short, sharp one; just as a long condition of poverty, and being kept low, will require Satan to use a different temptation from what would be suitable for some one heavy loss.

Now, one temptation which at times greatly vexes the sick is, *Envy at the condition of others* – envious thoughts about them; just as at times envy of the rich vexes the poor man, who sees even heedlessly thrown away what would be comfort, and almost wealth, to him.

This kind of thought sometimes comes very heavily upon us when we are laid aside.

Here are we in bed, or in our easy, or perhaps,

rather our *un*easy chair, and we get letters from friends saying that they are going here and there, and seeing this and that; or those around us are full of life and enjoyment; and the sun shines, and the breeze blows crisp; and while all life seems bright to them, alas! it seems to have very little to offer to us.

What can be more natural than that we should repine? What more so, than that we should envy those who have all that we have not, those to whom life is not one long discomfort, but apparently all sunshine?

We must expect thoughts like these to be raised in our minds from the very nature of our circumstances.

And what can such thoughts bring but great discomfort?

We need not, however, continue in this discomfort. We may meet these thoughts with other thoughts, which are comfortable ones.

And first of all, when I think how I am to be comforted under these circumstances, I ask myself, 'Who has appointed me my present lot? Who has sent me my illness? Is God in this matter? Have I distinct views upon this subject?

It is very unsafe to survey the lot of others, except in the light of God.

'A sound heart,' it says in Proverbs 14, 'is the life of the flesh, but envy the rottenness of the bones.'

Asaph fell into the trouble of which we are

speaking here. It pressed so hard upon him that his feet were almost gone, and his steps had well nigh slipped. It stirred very uncomely thoughts in him, and drew very uncomely words from him. He thought a great deal about it, and tried to understand all about it; but he confessed that it was too painful, too hard for him, until he went into the sanctuary; then he understood all about it. That 73rd Psalm forms a very useful study for all who are in like circumstances to Asaph.

To the sanctuary, that is to say, to God Himself, must you go, my sick friend, if you are to be comforted.

Art not Thou infinitely wise, O my God and Father? what! does my unbelieving heart want to make out that Thou hast made a mistake — a mistake in sending this illness to *me* at all, in its nature, its length, anything about it? Hast Thou come into contact with me in this matter for evil, with the design of hurting me? O my God, I will behold Thee in the sanctuary, not in the glass of my poor evil heart, where I would distort Thy image, but where Thou showest Thyself; and I believe that Thou art good, and good in the highest way to me.

And this is the God that has appointed to others their lot also. What I have, He gave me, even though it be pain; and what they have, He gave them, even though it be pleasure; shall He not do what He wills with His own?

But that would not be enough. I must believe

that infinite wisdom has been at work, to give me the thing best *for me*. Why it is best for me I know not; enough that, if it come from God, it must be so.

So then, I have nothing to do with the lot of others at all. It is as God has chosen to appoint it; and I am not to think that I can improve on it; it is all best as it is, best as it is, O my Father. I am comforted, because Thou who art all-wise and good hast settled my lot for me.

But there is another comfort.

Would the lot of these persons I am inclined to envy be the best for *me*? There are many things in the world which are good in themselves, but are not good for particular persons. Many dainty dishes are excellent for others, but not for me; and because I know that they are unsuitable for me, I avoid them.

And the lot of those we envy may on no account be a good one for us. It may be as bad for us as it is good for them. We each stand alone before God, with our peculiarities of character and temperament, with the temptations to which we are liable. We stand before Him in our individuality; and He deals with us one by one. Therefore, if I believe in God, I comfort myself, in the assurance that I have the lot that is best for *me*.

Why it should be best, as I have said, I cannot tell; that I must leave to God. I know that all connected with me lies naked and open before Him, with whom I have to do; and I know He is dealing with me as an individual; that my case stands as it were alone before Him.

I comfort myself, O my God, with the belief that Thou appointest what is best for me – for *me*!

Then we may ask ourselves the question – Is it indeed so happy with those we envy? Are we certain that in the spending of money, or in the going to and fro, or in enjoying one pleasure after another, people are indeed so happy as we, who cannot enter into these things, suppose? These things sparkle more, and make more noise, than enjoyments of a quieter kind; but so does the babbling brook with but little water, sparkle more, and make more noise as it breaks over the stones, than the deep waters which glide noiselessly in all their mighty power toward the sea.

How soon the pleasures which we envy come, and go! How soon they burn out! How many of them leave nothing but ashes behind! when the week of the gay ones and our week is ended, what have they had, so much more than we?

We put a false gloss on many things; and we may comfort ourselves with the thought that much which we fancied we had lost was nothing but just the painting of our own imagination.

We forget very often that there are different kinds of happinesses and pleasures; and our kind, perhaps, is not the least, or worst. If they have theirs, we have ours. We are different trees, and there hang upon us different fruits. If we think ourselves left without any good thing in our condition, no wonder if we are unhappy and discontented; for the Almighty has so constructed man that he never can be happy, as long as he thinks he is left without any good. The point is, to believe we have our good things as well as others have theirs; and if only we think, many of them will appear. 'There be many that say, Who will show us any good? Lord, lift Thou up the light of Thy countenance upon us. Thou hast put gladness in my heart, more than in the time that their corn and wine increased.' The Psalmist had peace – 'I will both lay me down in peace, and sleep, for Thou, Lord, only makest me dwell safely' [Psalm 8:6–9].

When you are seeking comfort from this source, ask yourselves this question, Have I discovered *all* the good that is incidental to my lot? Let us try to find out good things in our condition, and we shall be sure to do so. God hath set the one over against the other, it says in the Scripture; and if He has appointed the bitter, we may rest assured He has appointed some sweet with it.

Very often, we have to hunt for our blessings to find them. They are none the worse for that; unless the violet be the worse for having to be looked for amid the leaves.

In sickness, little mercies are as sweet and as really great to you, as very great things are to other people in health. Give a poor man £50 and he has as real a sense of wealth as a rich man if you give him £1,000. Moreover, he has as great enjoyment in settling how he will spend it, and in spending it. Enjoyment is enjoyment, whether it uses as its machinery what is great or small; and there may be as much enjoyment to you in sitting out in the open air quietly for an hour, as there is to another in a day's shooting, or fishing, or going on an excursion, or having some great pleasure. Things are, as they are to *us*; and you have your great pleasure, just as he has his. Ask God to show you the good things incidental to your lot. Believe that there are some, and look for them. It is astonishing how many things turn up, when they are regularly hunted for. There are sick men who have had as much real pleasure in being able to move a joint, as a school boy has had in winning the prize in athletic sports; to whom a mutton chop has been as dainty a treat as a Lord Mayor's feast.

Set about blessing-hunting, then, as soon as you can. Blessing-hunting is comfort-hunting. The fisherman may go out and catch nothing, the foxhunter may go out and have no find; but if you go out blessing-hunting, you must succeed.

Let others then go their way upon the path which God has appointed them; enough for you that it is not *your* path. Do not expect to find *their* things on *your* path; even as they are not to expect to find yours on theirs. They may be happy and useful in their lot, be you so in yours.

It is when we want to move outside our own spheres that we get discontented and envious and unhappy; and that we fail in what God has appointed for us.

And we must try not to be failures, but to be found at the last to have glorified God in our own sphere. We may be sure we shall do best for His glory and for our own happiness in the lot which infinite wisdom and love have pointed out for us.

8: A COMFORT IN OUR BEING
A TROUBLE TO OTHERS

All our trouble in time of illness does not come simply on our own account. Very often, our illness makes us sad on account of dear ones on whom we are made dependent, upon whom this illness must exercise some pressure. It will lay more upon them, perhaps more of our work; or at any rate it will take more of their time, perhaps of their means; and the thought of that is a great aggravation of our trouble.

It may be that such a thought as this comes from a proud heart; for there are some who would not be dependent upon others for any thing. And if this be the case, God will bring down this pride. It is not like Christ, not to be dependent upon any one for any thing. He was indebted to many, and for many things. There were women who ministered to Him of their substance. He was ready to be under obligation to the woman of Samaria for a cup of water; and to the man who owned the upper chamber for the use of it for the passover; and, no doubt, many a night's lodging had He, for which He thanked those who gave it to Him. There were those who took trouble about Him; and walking the earth as a man, with human needs, He was willing not only to give, but also to receive.

But perhaps, your trouble comes from a sensitive heart. Some people, no doubt, are not sensitive, but others are; and their state of illness generally makes them still more so. And under these circumstances, we may, and often do worry ourselves into a state of great misery.

Now what has our Comfort Book to say under these circumstances?

First of all, it says, Do your friends, and those who minister to you, consider you such a trouble as you fear yourself to be? Have you any reason to think they do?

It sometimes happens that we estimate things by our own sick querulousness, in which we count every thing a trouble; and then, as every thing is to us, every feather or straw a burden, so we think it is to them. To you, my sick friend, it may be a great burden even to hold up a book; it may tire you very much to walk a few steps; you cannot talk for five minutes at a time. But you must not measure your friends round about you by yourself. You and they are under different circumstances altogether; they do not make a burden of things, as you do. It is quite natural that you should make a burden of them, it is equally natural that they should not.

So here is a comfortable thought at the very outset. Your friends in health do not probably think you to be such a trouble at all.

But consider not only the health, but the love of those who minister to you.

You are probably attended to by some who love you from relationship; or, it may be, who are nothing at all to you in blood, but they have an affection for you; and in the power of that affection they serve. Now, love makes no account of trouble; on the other hand, it rejoices in opportunities of showing itself, and counts many a thing which is troublesome in itself, no trouble at all because of the one for whom it is done. Even the natural kindliness which we feel towards the sick, you must take into account. You would feel it towards others, they feel it towards you. It is the spirit in which a thing is done that very often determines the amount of trouble in it; and those who minister to you, do so in a loving spirit, and therefore they count their trouble small.

Then, there is another comfort. God will reward those who minister to us, for what they do for His sake. You must not think that those who are doing anything for you are doing so without any prospect of reward. Perhaps, you cannot give them much, or even anything; but there is One who notes all they do, and who in His own time and way will reward them. If you have a full belief in that, it will be a great comfort. We shall thus feel that we are not taking the labour of those who are kind to us, for naught. God will return it all many times into their bosom. And we must pray that He will do so. And in so praying, if we have any belief that our prayers are heard and answered, we shall find much comfort. Yes! we, even we, the poor helpless ones, who have but little to give, are blessing them; we are making a return to them. Your Father, who undertakes every thing for you, will be your paymaster as well as every thing else. Let your heart be comforted in the thought that, in His own way, He will repay all you owe.

Who knows how He will do this? And should we want to know? Faith is not always wanting to *know*. Perhaps others will do for those who are helping you, just as you have done for them. You may be sure that their time of need will come; and you may pray that, in that time of need, their want may be supplied. Pray in earnestness and faith; and then be comforted in the thought that you have blessed those who have ministered to you.

'But,' you say, 'it seems very humiliating, very sad, to be so dependent on others.'

Well, consider this. The law of dependence is to be found everywhere. We must all be dependent one upon another in some form. And you are only filling up one side of the law of dependence. God has appointed you to be the one to depend, even as He has appointed your kind friends to be the ones to be depended on. You are in your place in God's great plan; and perhaps you are the means He uses for giving your friends an opportunity of filling up the other side of the law of dependence, by ministering to you, and so receiving the blessing that belongs to ministry. Remember how Jesus came under this law, when He received the ministry of others; and how Paul did so; and in the history of the greatest men, instances are continually coming to light in which they did so also.

And now, it is a further comfort to think that, in many instances, we may save those who are in ministry to us.

In times of illness, wants, especially 'little wants,' are unfortunately many. Now, we may try and limit these wants. Sometimes, a little forethought will save those who wait on us a great deal of trouble. The sick-bed, or arm-chair, are not without their opportunities for thought-fulness and self-denial.

At any rate, we may limit our complaints. I do not mean to say that we should not ever tell sympathizing friends something of what we suffer; but we need not weary them with our complaints, as some people do. And it will be a comfortable feeling that we are sparing them a knowledge of *all* we are going through ourselves.

And then, we may return gratitude, and that shown and expressed; so that those around us will feel that we appreciate what they do for us. I do not believe in the silent system altogether. I think that the expression of gratitude gives pleasure; and that it encourages our friends, and makes them feel that their labour is not in vain; and it is a comfortable thought that we have *thus* much within our reach.

Here is another comfort. God gives to those who are willing to serve Him in ministry to the bodies of others, the feelings and the patience which are suitable to such a situation. There are many who are ministering to others in a strength not their own at all, but God's. Perhaps those who minister to you have such strength; if they have not, and you ask it for them, they will get it; and then the idea of 'trouble' will not easily come into their minds.

It is also a comfort that the feelings with which others minister to us, are often very much affected by what we are; and consequently in this matter of being a trouble to them, we have something in our power. We are not stretched upon our beds altogether helpless. If then we try to be cheerful, if we are grateful, if we show ourselves pleased, if we appreciate and make much of what is done for us, we shall make the task of those who minister to us lighter; and to be able to do that should be a comfort.

And think of this. Who knows what opportunities we may have, of repaying in the world to come the kindnesses which have been shown to us on our sick-beds. To go far into such a thought as this would no doubt be speculation; but it may be that, hereafter, when there will be an opportunity for the play of all the finer feelings of our nature, gratitude will not be left out.

If Jesus says, 'I was sick and ye visited me,' and because of that kindness repays a thousand-fold, we may rest assured that the followers will not be worse off than the Master.

We can see no reason why there should not be giving and receiving in heaven in all the interchange of love; we shall not consider it the highest happiness to keep every thing to ourselves. If there be holy relationships in heaven which have had their first germ and root on earth, we may well believe that that which exists between the one who ministers and the one who is ministered to will be one of them.

So then, be comforted even in being a burden to others. Sad as the thought is, it has its alleviations.

If the thought is a gracious and shrinking one, you may use all these consolations, and find blessing in them; but if the thought is a proud one, and you rebel at your helplessness, and are too proud to be dependent on any one; then God has made no provision for such thoughts; and the sooner you forsake them the better.

The waters of comfort cannot run up the hills of pride; they fall down into the valleys of humility. Here, as everywhere else, 'God resisteth the proud, but giveth grace to the humble.' We need not be down-hearted; even this phase of our affliction has its alleviations, and its comforts too.

9: A COMFORT IN FEAR THAT
THE AFFLICTION WILL BE LONG

I can sympathize with sufferers in their fear that their trial, whatever it is, will be long. This thought adds, I can quite believe, to your trouble. If only you could see an end of it, that would take away half the burden, but that is the very thing that you cannot do; and so, we must cast about for the comfort which belongs to this particular phase of your trial.

And there are comforts to be had; for the Holy One who allows your affliction to be long, has not ordained any state on this earth which is wholly comfortless.

The first grand comfort will come from living by the day. God meant us to live by the day. It was sin that brought in 'trouble about the future,' and distrust of God; and conjured up all sorts of fears and doubts and disbeliefs, to people the long weary time that it brings before the mind. God meant Adam to live by the day; and when he fed men Himself from heaven, He fed them by the day; and He says, 'Sufficient unto the day is the evil thereof;' and what we are to pray for is our daily bread. No power on earth will enable us to turn the page of to-morrow's life. 'Ye know not what shall be on the morrow.' If you want to be happy in a long affliction, and to go well through it, you must resolutely shut

your eyes to to-morrow. Let night be 'the death
of each day's life.'

God has mercifully cut up life into short pieces,
into days; if He had not done so, we must have
been overwhelmed. Now we know by every day's
experience that we can do what in the aggregate
is a great deal, if only we do it bit by bit. And it is
bit by bit that we are to bear our long affliction.
Never reach forth your hand for to-morrow's
trouble. Grace is only for to-day's. You should
not bring upon yourselves a need for which there
is no promise of supply.

Now, is it not a comfort that God does not
allow you to be overloaded? You may overload
yourself; and if you do, He will let the natural
consequence, in the way of a troubled mind,
come upon you; but if you are determined not
to overload yourself, be happy in the thought
that no one else can put too much on you.

Therefore you may say, 'How long the future
will be I know not; but I know that it will and
must be a future of *days*; and as my days, so also
shall my strength be.' [Deut. 33:25.]

Be comforted also with the thought that the
time of affliction is sometimes much shorter than
people expect. People who have looked forward
to being invalids for weeks, or months, or even
years, have been restored in a marvellous and
wholly unexpected way. It may be so with you.
You do not know what God has in store for you.
I remember a pious physician once saying, 'God

is often better to us than our fears,' and in that case it turned out to be so.

Perhaps, you may never be wholly raised up; well, even without this, there may be great blessing before you; you may be raised up to be ever so much better than you are now. Take some comfort out of the possibility of things. You do not know what God has still in store for you.

But suppose it should be His holy will that you remain as you are – an invalid, all your life; even here you need not be without comfort. The mighty power of habit will do much for you. From the habit of being on the sofa, or in bed, or being confined to the house, all these trials will be far less than they would have been, if they came only at intervals, and for short periods.

It is also a comfort to think that, no matter how long our trial may be, it will never be too long for God's intention. 'So far shalt thou go, and no farther,' is what He has said to the waves of the sea; and though they may rage horribly, yet they can never overpass the sandy limit they have been assigned. And, 'So far shalt thou go and no farther,' is what He has said with reference to our trial. So then, God's intention will be in this trial as much this day twelvemonth, or ten years, as it is to-day; and that being the case, we must not think that we shall have any meaningless trial; any without *The Presence*.

Woe indeed would it be to us, if our trials could outlive the continuance of God with us;

then indeed, we may look forward to cheerless days, and dark and fearful nights, to loneliness and faintings; but length will be met by length, the length of our trial by that of His presence. What we *have* experienced in this way we *shall* experience. He says, 'I am with you always, even unto the end.' [Matt. 28:20.]

It is another comfort to reflect that the length of the trial shall not outstrip our requirements.

Why we need this or that affliction, we do not always know. The requirements of each man are known only to God. Sometimes we do see these requirements, and then we are apt to deal very superficially with them; we think that a little trial works a great reformation, or teaches a great lesson. But God goes to the root. He knows what we need, and what He is doing; and every day that we are to have of this trial, if we use it aright, will be filling up some need of our soul.

Comfort yourself also with the assurance that the trial will not be too long for your blessing.

God will not send trial without the intention of blessing; therefore, where the trial is great, we may be sure that the blessing intended is great also. If the trial were to be allowed to lengthen itself out beyond the possibility of fruit bearing, it would become simply an evil, an objectless infliction. Therefore, say to yourself, 'This day's trial could not be spared; God has still further blessing in store for me.' To be able to reason thus, you must, of course, believe in God, and that practically; and if you do not, I cannot write a Comfort book at all for you. I am helpless to comfort without God.

And now remember this further. Your trial cannot be longer than the lasting power of God's faithfulness, and mercy, and patience, and power. He will be true to you all through it. His patience will not be exhausted, His power will not come short. You will never be left without God. He will be in all your to-morrows, even as He is in your to-day, and has been in all your yesterdays.

Moreover, you shall not be without alleviations. It shall not be all pain, all depression, all weariness, never a sun-gleam, never a smile. The alleviations may come by small instruments, and they may seem trivial to those in health; but the point is not what they are to others, but what they are to you. God is not straitened in His resources, He can make plenty of gourds to grow, plenty of chinks through which the sunbeams can penetrate, plenty of sunbeams to come in. He can put a pleasure and a power into little things, which will absolutely surprise you. What is nothing in health, He will make very precious in illness. Say then to yourself: There are to be alleviations all the way through; never a day without something comforting; and this being the case I will look out for it, and hail it, and use it when it comes.

Believe that long afflictions have their peculiar meaning and blessing.

Believe that yours must have.

Be sure that they have their peculiar place in God's kingdom; and then, surely, you would not deliberately wish to have them shortened, against the will of God, and take all the consequences.

You cannot see how tremendous in the matter of loss these consequences may be; do not risk them; leave all with God, who knows all.

'Our light affliction which is but for a moment, worketh for us a far more exceeding and eternal weight of glory.' Blessed is he that endureth; in the end there is the yielding of the peaceable fruit.

If now we have a look forward, by and by we shall have a look backward, upon all the way by which we have been led. Even now, when we look back upon what we would call long periods, how short they seem, although they are comparatively recent! How much shorter will they appear when they are looked back upon from the stand-point of eternity!

'Weeping may endure for a night, but joy cometh in the morning.'

Henceforth then, let the man who fears that his trial will be long determine to keep himself to to-day; let him shut himself in by to-night; it is not long to to-night, he can hold out thus far; and let the morrow take care of itself.

Who knows what deliverances are before him? Who knows what alleviations?

Who knows what his sickness is working for him, in the shape of an exceeding weight of glory?

There is an end appointed; each day passed is one day less for endurance.

But come what may, my God will be faithful to me all through; and will hold me by my right hand, even to the end.

10: A COMFORT IN THE THOUGHT THAT WE SHALL HAVE TO BE ALONE

The sick have often to be much alone. While others are going to and fro in the various businesses of life, their lot is to be alone, with their thoughts, perhaps, turned in upon themselves; with no apparent fellowship, save that of their pains. Sometimes, sick people have no friends who can be with them; and sometimes, friends can stay with us only a very little while; for life is busy, and there are few who have not work pressing upon them which must be done.

It is no wonder, if some heart-sinkings accompany the loneliness of illness. Man was made by God for companionship, and not for solitude. It is not sinful, it is quite natural that we should feel distressed at this thought of solitude.

But there is much comfort to be had, if we think that solitude is far from being all evil; for it has its good things.

The earth's surface, peopled with life, with waving trees, and grazing oxen, and busy man, has unnumbered forms of beauty; but away, down in the ocean depths, is beauty too; there are to be seen, in its corals and shells, and what we call weeds, and in its living inhabitants, many forms of beauty – unlike, indeed, to those which belong to the surface of the earth, but beauty, both in form and colour, still.

Let us now search in our lonely time (or rather in our times of being alone – for we may be 'alone' without being 'lonely') for some of its beautiful things; let us draw our comforts from itself.

Look first at your Lord and Master, Jesus Christ; He was alone. He was alone in His great temptation. In all that wilderness time He saw no human face, He heard no human voice. He, with man's sympathies, and man's needs, was cut off from men. The evil one came to Him; but as regards human fellowship – alone!

And you have fellowship with His suffering. Strengthen yourself in the honour of being in some small measure even as Christ was.

When we go into the crowd, we must expect the temptations of the crowd; and when into solitude, then the temptations of solitude; but, in each case, we may have fellowship with Jesus.

And Jesus was alone from all human applause. In one sense, He was always alone from it; for He was out of sympathy with it; but He actually withdrew from it – from time to time He was by 'Himself alone.'

We think that there are some sustainments in human applause, and so there are; but they are sustainments which do not penetrate the depths of our nature, and which can never hold us up to do anything abidingly great. In missing them, we miss less than we suppose. Human applause did not carry Jesus through anything; what He did, He did without it; and we may do the like.

Here, then, are you in fellowship with Jesus; throw yourself into oneness with Him; and though none may appreciate your patience, none understand your position, as it was with Him, so shall it be with you. Your circumstances are like His; He will make you, in your measure, like Himself.

He was alone in His agony. Those who might at least have watched with Him, slept. Heaven only heard His groans, and saw His bloody sweat; and when He was strengthened, it was not by human sympathy, but by an angel from heaven.

We may have to be alone in much of our pain. It would be a great solace to us to have a hand to press. It would be even a comfort to feel that our sigh, or our groan, or our long-drawn breath, fell upon some sympathetic ear, and awoke an echo in some sympathetic heart; but that cannot be; we must be alone. Then let us say, 'I, in my small measure, am even as Thou wast, O my Lord.'

Jesus was very often alone, in want of sympathy, and in the loneliness of not being understood. Depend upon it, however little sympathy you may have, you have more than He had; however often you may be misunderstood, you are not misunderstood as often as He was. You may often say to yourself, 'Ah, how much better off am I than Thou wast, O my Lord.' And Jesus will allow us to be one with Him. Though we cannot enter into the depths of His suffering in any one form of it, still we can be in fellowship with it as regards 'kind;' and to be in fellowship with Him will brighten any lonely hour.

But *being alone* is not of necessity *loneliness*. We cannot help being alone; the circumstances in which we are placed probably necessitate that we should be so; but much of the feeling of loneliness may come simply from ourselves. Jesus, when most alone as regards the world, was in communion with the Father. To be alone in the fearful sense of the word is one thing; to be alone with God is another.

Encourage yourself in the thought of 'a presence', and that presence – your Father's. And that presence you will never have without His voice speaking to you, and without your voice being drawn out to respond to His.

But there is another source, none the less real because it is lower, from which you may derive much happiness. Your mind, your imagination, may people your solitude, and do much for you. Many persons have their solitude thus furnished so richly that it might be said that they are never so little alone as when alone.

Our sick-bed, or our sofa, or arm-chair, need not be the poor limit of our sphere of life. We may leave them all in a moment; we may leave them far behind. Our bodies, no doubt, are kept in the chamber of weakness; but our bodies are not ourselves. We have that within us which can people our present abode, where we dwell alone, with the hopes, and thoughts, and beings of the other life. Our imagination is for use, as well as everything else. Let it be sanctified, and kept within its proper bounds, and it will bring us blessing. Let us often in our 'alone times' think of the holy angels who are round about us; of the activity and everlasting health of that land whither we are going. Let us try to live amid the activities of another life, though we be withdrawn from those of this. Thus, we may have many friends – thus, we need never be without friends.

It will also be a comfort to us, if we can see that this estate of being alone may be a very good one indeed. We never can find any happiness in a condition which we deliberately consider, from its very nature, to be destitute of good.

Now, there is very often much help heavenward, in our being alone. So much is there, indeed, that our Father often sets His children alone that they may be helped.

There is great undistractedness in being alone. We hear Christians continually complaining of the distractions of life; but there is little to distract in the chamber of illness. The calm of standing on one side of life's road, and under the shade, is ours. Much, no doubt, which might be procured by active exertion we have not; but much of the spirit-wearing which is incidental to procuring it, we are also spared. A blessed calm ought to be ours. If it be not, we have lived below the privileges of our estate; and are dragging into our sphere that which belongs to another. Accept your calm as a blessing.

And who has such opportunities of speaking with God, and hearing from Him, as you have? You may be almost like Moses in the mount.

Consider too that great things have come out of solitude. Great men have been fashioned by it. It is the very nursery of meditation and thought; and what is man without thought? But do not let your thought take a wrong direction. Do not let it turn in too much upon yourself. Balance the inward with the outward; the way to prevent our being overwhelmed by considering what we are, is by considering at the same time what God is.

And, if possible, balance thought by action. The work of the sick-room and the sick man, cannot in the nature of things be great; possibly, it may not even be very useful. But what may not be very much in itself, may be a great deal to you; therefore, as far as you can, always set out your day's little work, and you shall have the pleasure which always follows upon accomplishment – upon work done. Do not compare your work with that of others. You have nothing to do with theirs; be happy in your own, and be content.

It is, perhaps, a poor way to derive comfort for ourselves by reflecting upon the miseries of others;

still, it will surely make us somewhat happier in our condition of being alone, if we remember that there are many who would give much of what they have, if only they could be somewhat more alone. Driven hither or thither, in the way of business or pleasure, or it may be family care, they long for quiet which they cannot have.

And there are many whom we perhaps envy, who are really alone amid a thousand. Theirs is loneliness indeed – a solitude not of place, but of heart. From this we may be free. There is no reason why the quiet place in which we have been set should not be a place of cheerfulness, our few friends and their few visits, and our own many thoughts, and God's many communings, making our wilderness and solitary place glad, and our desert to rejoice and blossom as the rose.

11: A COMFORT IN OUR FEARS
THAT WE SHALL FAIL AND
DISHONOUR GOD AT THE LAST

This fear, which we are about now to glance at, is a very natural one. In one sense, comfort may be had from ever having had such a fear at all. For though the believer should be above all such fears, still this one must have sprung out of an honest and good heart. It is only in such that it could root itself; it is only such that it can disturb.

To a great extent, the fear is in itself a natural one. When we look back on the past history of our life, what meets us but a sad record of failures? Where we thought ourselves strongest, there we have proved ourselves weakest; where we thought we had done best, we have done worst; and we know enough of ourselves in the past to make us believe that we are capable of any folly or failure for the future.

In this case, the same evil which produces our trouble may produce also the antidote to it. For out of this may come a holy distrust of self, a safe and profitable feeling, one altogether distinct from any distrust of God; one which, on the other hand, makes us throw ourselves upon God, and in so doing, find peace.

The fear, however, springs, it may be, more from the feeling that the unknown lies before us – the unknown as to the amount both of our temptation, and our weakness. The unknown we almost always fear. And yet, with the unknown before us, we must always live. No man can tell what the morrow will bring forth.

There are two ways of meeting the unknown – either by not thinking about it at all, or by thinking and leaving it all to God.

We may, indeed, be very weak in our last hours, weaker than we have ever been in our lives before; we may also be more sorely tempted. If so, as we have met many unknowns in the past, when they developed themselves, so we may believe that we shall meet this unknown when it comes also. Distance, it is said, lends enchantment to the view; distance lends terror also; God sees the future both of our weakness and of our temptation; and when they come, we shall find that He has come with them.

The Word of God is intended to be, not a fear-creating, but a fear-dispelling Word. No doubt it warns us about ourselves – our own weakness, and nothingness, and entire liability to fall – but this is only to prevent our being set on the wrong basis of self and our own strength. 'Let him that thinketh he standeth take heed lest he fall.' But once off your own basis, there is no more mention of weakness. 'Be strong in the Lord, and in the power of His might' is the word. 'The Lord is my strength, and my song, and He is become my salvation.' Greater is He that is with us, than they that be against us.

One of the uses of 'the Word' is to lift us out of self-strength, to put us on new standing-ground altogether, to take us out of the land of fears, and set our feet in the land of faith.

In one sense, then, these fears are right, so far as they come from an estimate of self; in another they would be wrong and, like all wrong things, must exercise a disturbing influence. That disturbing influence God wills not for us; and so we must get well on to the standing-ground of simple faith, where we shall find Him; and in Him the One who is to dispel our fears.

Sometimes, we fear we shall fail in faith, as though when it came to the trial of our long-professed trust we may be found wanting; but faith is the gift of God; and why should our Father take away His gift from us *then*, at the very moment when we need it most?

Sometimes, we think we shall fail in patience – that either pain or weariness of body may make us say, or do, what is unseemly, and prevent our lying still in a Father's hand.

Then again, we think we shall come short in comfort – that those comforts which we now have will be withdrawn; or that, even if they are there, we shall not be able to make them our own; and so we go on, until we see the future all wrapped in gloom.

Let us put a stop at the very beginning to such thoughts as these. They have a wonderful tendency to spread and darken the whole of our

horizon; we thus make a black future for ourselves. This is not God's future for us; it is the
future of our own faithless hearts.

Now, what we are to do, is this. We must
leave the future to God — our future must be a
God-made, God-wrought one. Our comfortable
considerations must come from thoughts connected with Him.

And take this as a first comfortable thought:
If we have committed God's honour to Himself
in this matter, He will guard it. Nowhere can
God's honour be so well guarded as in His own
keeping. Therefore, we may say, 'Work for Thine
honour's sake, O my Father, O Lord most Mighty,
in keeping me in my last hours, with their weaknesses and temptations, whatever they may be.
Do not let me dishonour Thy promises, or Thy
faithfulness, by distrusting them; hold me at
that time in the hollow of Thine own hands.'
And God's honour will be dear to Him; and He
will remember the trust we repose in Him; and
although we may have forgotten it, He will not;
and His strength will be made perfect in our
weakness.

Consider, too, another comfortable thought,
'Is not the last the same as the first to Him?'
If, to His own honour, He first of all drew us forth
from the world, and into communion with Himself, for what purpose is it but that we should be
His? Is the last keeping harder than the first
drawing? We have already had experience of

His power; we may be sure that His hand is not shortened that it cannot save.

Consider that it will be the same God that will be in our last weakness, as has been in our many past weaknesses. All we shall have to do will be to repose in His arms. That is to us the gain of His strength. It is no use to us that He is strong, unless He is so for us.

So that what we are to do is to see God Himself entirely on this scene – to see Him in action on our behalf; to look upon ourselves not as bearers, but as those who are to be borne.

And be sure that this tenderness of heart which is felt as regards one's dishonouring God in any way at the last – by unbelief, or fear, or in any other way – is in itself a blessed sign and witness that this shall not come to pass. God will be tender of those who are tender of His honour. They who will to glorify Him shall glorify Him. Perhaps, we shall say, as we lie passive in His hand, leaving Him to undertake for us, 'Thou hast kept the good wine until now'; and in the strengthening and exhilaration thereof, our last words on earth shall be speaking good of His name; and we shall, being dead, yet speak, and tell others to fear no evil; for in the last hour God will be with them; His rod and His staff will comfort them.

12: A COMFORT IN THE THOUGHT OF OUR DEPARTURE HENCE

I put it thus, 'departure hence.' I might have said 'Death;' but we invest that word with such a cloud of terrors, with so many false thoughts that I shall call what is known by the name of 'Death,' as simply 'Departure.'

All sorts of gloomy thoughts come into the mind by nature, when we think of leaving this world. We associate it with pain and distress and separation and loneliness and strangeness and fear of the unknown. Many, even of God's children, need much comfort in view of this parting from earth.

One great comfort will be to believe that the best arrangement is made for everything connected with it. Not arrangement by ourselves, or any near and dear to us; but by the One who from the beginning has arranged all things. He who has ordered the movements of all the heavenly bodies, and the relationships of all earthly things – times and seasons, summer and winter, cloud and sunshine – He who is so active in all things connected with life, is equally active in all things connected with what we call Death.

My first great comfort then is from thoughts that the best arrangement is made for everything connected with my departure hence.

The needs of that time may be many; they can be known to but One, that is, to God; and, He

who knows the needs is the One to provide the
supply.

The little infant that is sent into this world, so
strange to it, has everything provided for it by the
One who sent it; those who are sent by the same
One into another world shall not be worse off.

And if God is arranging, we may surely leave
it all to Him. He is the One who knows the needs
of the road we have to travel; we are warranted
in leaving it all. Much of our trouble in life comes
from the workings of unbelief, which makes us
want to do all for ourselves, rather than leave
God to do all. But, under no circumstances can
we do anything here; and, therefore, to trouble
ourselves about so doing, is folly indeed.

Be still, in the consciousness that you are
arranged for. Trouble yourself neither about the
great things nor the little of that journey; your
Father's mind has settled all about them.

That Father is God Himself. All His power
and goodness and wisdom and love have been at
work. He has been working in Christ. He who
Himself departed, knows all about departures;
and so we may say with the Psalmist, 'Yea,
though I walk through the valley of the shadow
of death I will fear no evil; for Thou art with
me; Thy rod and Thy staff they comfort me.'

It is the believer's privilege to refuse to think
about anything connected with death, to leave
it all, to lie still, to believe that God will be equal
to Himself, that there will be no miscarrying,

no coming short to us of His purposes of love; and, surely, there is no small comfort here.

Next: as to our thoughts on this subject.

Things often become almost substantial to us by the way in which we think of them, and by the amount of the thought we give them.

Thus it is that the way in which men think of Death makes it so gloomy. They connect it with pain, and rending of soul and body, and the loneliness, and coldness, and outside-ness of the grave, and with many such sad thoughts as these.

But, let us train our minds to something very different from this.

There is no such rending asunder of the soul and body, as we suppose. How many deaths are painless! how many are mere goings to sleep! how, over and over again, have we seen that, when the time of departure is drawing near, there comes with it a strange sense of resigna-tion, of peacefulness, a kind of charm seems to take possession of the one about to depart!

No doubt, there are many cases which people describe as 'dying hard;' but, in the first place, physicians assure us that, what seems to us to be suffering is none to the apparent sufferer; and even if it were, it is probably no more, if as much, as many a pain already endured over and over again.

Let us hope to *sleep* in Jesus; to depart, even in this respect, in peace. We know not the moment when we lose ourselves, to the outer world, in sleep; then we become practically dead to it; we shall not know the moment when we go hence.

I sometimes think that the departure of the soul from the body may be more gradual than we suppose – it may *fleet away* more than we think.

Sailing away to a far distant land, as the shores of this country gradually became dim, I remember thinking, 'Perhaps thus will it be with me when I die.' The soul may be loosening itself from its earthly tenement for a while before; and, when the time comes, there may be but a very slender thread to break – yes, perhaps nothing which can be described by the word 'breaking' at all, a receding of this world's shore, an indistinctness of the objects on this strand, an increasing distinctness of those on the other. I seldom cross to the Isle of Wight, but that I think of this. I see the shore I left gradually growing dim, and the one I am going to gradually becoming clear, and I say, 'Perhaps it will be thus with me when I depart.' Let us say to ourselves, 'I shall *sleep* in Jesus.'

Nor need we fear the strange, the unknown. The little babe who comes into this new world has no fear – all is strange, all unknown; but it is not born into any fears on this account.

Let us try to surround our departing time with such thoughts as these. We are going to our Father. We are provided for by our Father. Our Father is in all. We are going to a place, to friends, to life. A home, and not a grave, is the true ending of our earthly life; we depart not to be, as we say, 'dead,' but really to live.